WORLD PROBLEMS

Emma Mary Hall

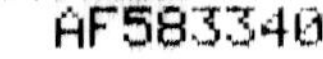

CURRENCY PRESS
The performing arts publisher

MELBOURNE THEATRE COMPANY

CURRENT THEATRE SERIES

First published in 2024
by Currency Press Pty Ltd,
Gadigal Land, Suite 310, 46–56 Kippax Street, Surry Hills, NSW 2010, Australia
enquiries@currency.com.au
www.currency.com.au

in association with Melbourne Theatre Company

Typeset by Brighton Gray for Currency Press.
Printed by Fineline Print + Copy Services, Revesby, NSW.
Cover image shows Carly Sheppard, Melbourne Theatre Company 2024;
photo by Jo Duck.

The publisher has made every reasonable effort to obtain permission of the copyright holder whose work is reproduced in these pages. Any enquiries should be addressed to the publisher at the above address.

Currency Press acknowledges the Traditional Owners of the Country on which we live and work. We pay our respects to all Aboriginal and Torres Strait Islander Elders, past and present.

A catalogue record for this
book is available from the
National Library of Australia

Contents

EMMA MARY HALL is an award-winning writer, performer and theatre-maker based in Victoria. *World Problems* is her debut with Melbourne Theatre Company. She has written three solo works (*We May Have to Choose*, *Ode to Man* and *World Problems*), all of which have earned multiple awards and/or presentation tours nationally and internationally. *Ode to Man* is published by Playlab. Emma has also directed two productions: *Breeders* (La Mama Theatre, 2021) and *Show Cat! Sleep Faster!* (VCA, 2020). She co-devised *After Joan* with third year performing arts students at Federation University (2024) and has worked as assistant director and/or dramaturg on several independent theatre productions around Melbourne. As a writer, Emma is interested in the ways in which the individual imagination is governed or shaped by broader social norms, and in the essential role theatre plays in helping us to experience and negotiate a shared truth.

What is original does not come from absolute blank nothing ('oblivion'), but from an electromagnetic tenderness—from remembering, not forgetting [...] *Earth needs this tenderness—I think there is some kind of fusion between tenderness and sadness, joy, yearning, longing, horror (tricky one), laughter, melancholy and weirdness. This fusion is the feeling of ecological awareness.*

—Letter 8, Timothy Morton,
Björk's letters with Timothy Morton (2015)
http://www.dazeddigital.com/music/gallery/20196/7/bjork-s-letters-with-timothy-morton

Each time a story helps me remember what I thought I knew, or introduces me to new knowledge, a muscle critical for caring about flourishing gets some aerobic exercise [...] *Each time I trace a tangle and add a few threads that first seemed whimsical but turned out to be essential to the fabric, I get a bit straighter that staying with the trouble of complex worlding is the name of the game of living and dying well together on terra.*

—Donna Haraway (2016)
Staying with the Trouble

Writer's Note

When I wrote *World Problems* I was trying to work out how, as an artist, to respond to the greatest existential crisis my culture has ever known. I say this as a white woman; Indigenous peoples of Australia have lived through environmental and societal collapse many times over. Indigenous Australians survived the ice age. I did not.

I am a solitary creature. I think more than I act. My private daydreams are as essential to me as water, and I get overwhelmed by the cacophony of the public sphere. But still, I watch for signs and permissions from others to help me decide a right way to live. I know that climate change demands all of us to move in the same direction. It requires deep and profound shifts in our thinking around privilege, reward, personal freedom, future, safety and death.

So I guess this monologue is my attempt to sift through all that. How could I make a solo show about a problem so essentially collective? I decided to try to map out a future for myself, not using a fictional world to imagine apocalypse, but using my own known reality. My life.

World Problems was written seven years ago and revised only slightly in early 2024. Seven years is about the time it takes to replace and renew all the cells in the human body. This seems fitting.

Over that time, *World Problems* has had several outings. It first emerged on a Cultureland residency in Amsterdam in 2017–18. Cultureland was a program funded privately by the incredible Maud Aarts and Dagobert Bergmans, providing artists with unfettered time and space to develop projects at the nexus of culture and nature. I had a place to stay and months to dream and write. Maud and Dagobert: I love you.

World Problems went on to be performed by me twice, once in Amsterdam in 2018 on the invitation of the wonderful Berith Danse at Oostblok Theatre, and then in an independent season at fortyfivedownstairs in Melbourne in 2019.

In 2023, when Jeremy Rice at Melbourne Theatre Company approached me about programming it for their Education season, I laughed. I had thought by writing so closely to my own life there was no way it could be performed by anyone else. *But it's my life*, I thought. *I am so ordinary.*

I am excited to witness the 2024 Melbourne Theatre Company production, performed by the incomparable Carly Sheppard and directed by the incisive, loving, joyful Cassandra Fumi. I know that Carly and Cassandra, working with the incredible creatives on this team, will make something celebratory, silly, surprising and hopefully transformative.

My deep gratitude to the talented and inspiring creatives who have worked on *World Problems* across its seasons. This World includes you: Asha Bee Abraham, Dann Barber, Prue Clark, Fleur Dean, Susie Dee, Cassandra Fumi, Harrie Hogan, Piper Huynh, Annah Jacobs, Nicki Jam, Rachel Lee, Rachel Lewindon, Olivia Monticciolo, Shae Neal, Sarah Nixon, Bridie Noonan, Amelia Jean O'Leary, Carly Sheppard, SS.Sebastian, Jasna Veličković and Mark Wilson.

My thanks and love also to Sam George and Nicola Gunn, two artists who remind me always why and how (invoking Donna Haraway my hero) 'to stay with this trouble'. xxxxx

World Problems was presented by Melbourne Theatre Company at Southbank Theatre, The Lawler, on 3 May 2024 with the following list of cast and creatives:

PERFORMER	Carly Sheppard

Writer, Emma Mary Hall
Director, Cassandra Fumi
Set & Costume Designer, Dann Barber
Lighting Designer, Harrie Hogan
Composer & Sound Designer, Rachel Lewindon
Movement Consultant, Amelia Jean O'Leary

Melbourne Theatre Company acknowledges the Boon Wurrung and Wurundjeri Woi Wurrung peoples of the Kulin Nation, the traditional custodians of the land on which we work, create and gather. We pay our respects to all First Nations people, their Elders past and present, and their enduring connections to Country, knowledge, and stories. As a Company we remain committed to the invitation of the Uluru Statement from the Heart and its call for voice, truth and treaty.

Carly Sheppard in rehearsal for MTC's production of WORLD PROBLEMS. *(Photo: Tiffany Garvie)*

Carly Sheppard and director Cassandra Fumi in rehearsal for MTC's production of WORLD PROBLEMS. *(Photo: Tiffany Garvie)*

Carly Sheppard in rehearsal for MTC's production of World Problems. *(Photo: Tiffany Garvie)*

Carly Sheppard and movement consultant Amelia Jean O'Leary in rehearsal for MTC's production of World Problems. *(Photo: Tiffany Garvie)*

Carly Sheppard in rehearsal for MTC's production of World Problems. *(Photo: Tiffany Garvie)*

CHARACTERS

PERFORMER

NOTE ON STAGE DIRECTIONS

World Problems is a show about life. About how we experience the world through (within?) a human body. About breath.

Perhaps the most important stage direction is: be present at all times.

Perhaps another direction is: perform some kind of constant, honest, physical action throughout.

It is up to you to decide what this action might be. Verbs that could be helpful when making your choice: building, interacting, creating, connecting, weaving, destroying, rebuilding.

Work is important. I imagine the action to be Sisyphean, in that it will never end. But I also think it could be nice if it offered us a sense of achievement and completion, however fleeting.

When I first performed *World Problems*, I built a trampoline as I spoke, slotting a metal frame together and hooking tarpaulin into springs. It took me fifty-five minutes.

Then I jumped on it.

This play text went to press before the end of rehearsals and may differ from the play as performed.

1.

I remember, one time, I was ten years old. And I was sitting in a circle of girls. One of them was explaining that there are two holes for a woman, one that you pee through and one that you bleed through.

Another time I turned away from a new girl at school who asked me if she could sit with us at lunchtime. She had oily hair, and an ugly backpack, and I had already been nice too many times that day, so I said no.

Actually now that I think about it, I didn't even say no, I just turned my back on her and kept talking and hoped she would disappear.

I remember I used to sit in the hot water closet next to my bedroom when I was a child. I would shut the door and listen to the darkness.

I remember in Year Three someone asked my classmate Daniel, who was from Mauritius in Africa, what it was like to be covered in poo.

I remember my father crying during his divorce, I'd never seen a man as big and strong as him double over, the way he did. I also remember him yelling 'YOU IDIOT GET OUT OF IT, GET OUT OF IT YOU BLOODY *LITTLE* ***<u>TOAD</u>***' when one of the opposition players tackled an All Black on the TV. That's the New Zealand Rubgy Union team, the All Blacks. They're not all black.

I remember watching the snot that my father picked from his nose and rolled into a tiny little ball and flicked onto the carpet one day, on his way to doing something else, absentmindedly, like it didn't really exist.

I remember the birthday cakes my mother would bake, especially a teddy bear one with chocolate butter icing and chocolate sprinkles for the fur, which was my favourite.

I remember a girl called Samantha who would come to my birthday parties, she had bright-white hair like a myth and she always smelled of urine. She lived in the caravan park around the corner from my house, it was called Levi Caravan Park, it was where the Snowtown Killers lived for a while, they killed twelve people, not in the caravan park, and the movie they made about those guys was actually filmed in Smithfield Plains, which is thirty kilometres away, not close at all.

I remember the dog we owned who lived outside and even when she was old and slow, she would get very anxious if we tried to bring her inside to sit by the fire at night.

I remember the cat we had that was killed out of the blue, by a car right outside our house. I remember looking at the skin that had been whipped off his face and the brightness of his gums and his snarl. His body stiff like this.

This is the cat that I think of when I have to answer those personal security questions on websites, you know, when they ask you the name of your first pet, even though he wasn't technically my first pet, I had had many pets by then including two rabbits and another cat and the dog I just told you about.

But I choose to use this cat's name on those websites. I miss him very much. Henry.

I remember dressing up and playing shop with my best friend Clare, we met on a slide in a playground when I was four. She had a tiny little face and a huge brown teddy bear bigger than her head and she used to cry a lot. One day we made a movie together in my father's home office about two chairs who decided to get married, we had to use chairs in the film because we didn't know any actors and it didn't matter because all they had to do was stand at the altar. The movie was called George and Charlie. I don't remember who wore the dress, whether it was George or Charlie. No-one will ever see that movie, we recorded it on VHS.

I remember the man who ran the fish and chip shop around the corner from my Mother's house when I was at high school. He sold the best hot chips I'd ever eaten and for only two dollars I would get enough for a whole meal. He was always playing Elvis records. He had huge sideburns.

'They say Elvis is dead!' he would yell to whoever was in line. 'But they're WRONG. He's alive and well and working in a fish and chip shop in Adelaide, South Australia!'

I remember having no boobs and this went on for many years, for ages, like forever. I remember having no boyfriend and this is still going on. I remember my first pair of glasses and I remember the ulcers I got from my braces.

I remember wearing waistcoats and matching shorts. I remember being teased for that. I remember puffy sleeves, ballet shoes, glitter, spandex, corduroy suit jackets previously worn by men.

I remember not remembering.

I remember panic attacks, and success, and Year Twelve exam results in the mail.

I remember a young man from Madrid behind a podium in Melbourne talking about the economic meltdown in Spain, years after it had happened, and only then did I realise I'd barely even noticed it at the time.

I remember the morning after nine-eleven. Our lecturer asked the whole class to stand for a minute's silence and this was the first time I had ever done anything like that, for people who lived in America. I remember her telling us that there was going to be a war.

I remember a famous anthropologist coming to speak to that same class. The anthropologist drew two huge overlapping circles on the white board in this great big lecture theatre and she told us that before her research on Indigenous cultures in the Australian desert, anthropologists had only ever talked about one of those circles. The one where the men lived.

She said that all she did to get noticed was talk about the other circle.

I remember moving to Canberra on the weekend of their worst bushfire of all time, driving uphill with ash falling on my windscreen.

I remember the times I saw my mother cry. I remember lying on the pavement at three a.m., after kissing a boy I shouldn't have. I remember myself. I remember myself. I remember getting drunk. I remember a floral dress I used to wear. I remember my favourite pair of black high heels. I remember phoning boys on a landline. I remember the yellow pages, and I remember looking myself up in the phone book, which was white. I remember running away from him down the street. I remember walking away from him down the street. I remember wondering if it was abuse, this thing he was doing to me.

I remember paying seventy-five dollars a week in rent. Seventy-five dollars a week. A WEEK. And I lived in a beautiful three bedroom house with wooden floorboards and a backyard and it was thirty minutes walk from the centre of town. I lived there with a young man called Johnny who wore glasses, and was rarely at home, and could only cook one thing—spaghetti—and I remember he had a big penis, but I never had sex with him or even saw him with his clothes off, so it's strange that I know that about him. His …

I remember the first time I had sex.

I remember reading about feminist cyborgs before I'd ever been naked with anyone. I remember getting locked in a library at Melbourne University with a handsome man from Europe. Nothing happened. I remember an Elton John concert where he wore bright green and sang about crocodiles, and I fell asleep on my father's lap in the cold.

I remember reading about the birth of the internet. I don't remember the first time I used the internet. I remember my first Nokia. I don't remember my first smart phone. I remember creating an email account. I remember my first kiss. I remember I used to be happier.

I remember talking to my best friend on the internet after too many beers. We argued, I think. I mean, I think it was an argument. But sometimes it isn't so easy to know, is it, on the internet.

I remember the bike I used to ride. I remember the eighties. I remember watching television, my nose pressed up against the screen. *Home and Away. A Country Practice. It's a Knockout.* I remember hating walnuts.

I remember caring about things. I remember seeing a future.

I remember believing good things were to come.

I remember taking magic mushrooms at a friend's thirtieth and immediately taking myself straight home to bed. I remember missed calls from the boy who'd given me the magic mushrooms that night on my phone screen.

I remember my phone screen.

I remember my passcode. I remember my first address.

I remember the reindeer I made out of coloured fabric for the Christmas card design competition I won at primary school. I remember winning the Christmas card design competition at primary school with my design of a reindeer made out of coloured felt fabric.

I remember having to share the winning with three other kids who also did designs, and they put all of our designs together on the same card so my reindeer only took up the bottom right hand corner, and I remember being really pissed off about that. Because my reindeer design was by far the best design, everyone else drew shitty pictures in crayon, but I used coloured felt fabric that was then photographed, and the use of textiles meant the colours came out much clearer and more vivid in the printing so it was in a completely different league from those other crayon drawings, it was simply *better* than anything you could ever make with a crayon. So much better. It was magnificent.

I still think this.

I remember winning a milkshake maker from a cereal box competition. I remember winning a stuffed toy at a fairground. I remember screwing up a certificate in Primary School because I was bored with being told I was good at things. I remember being good at things. I remember being good. I remember bleeding on my school uniform. I don't remember my first tampon. I do remember my hairy legs.

I remember the fall of the Berlin Wall, people seemed happy about it, on the TV.

Chernobyl: I remember watching the news about it, I was only a child and it sounded bad but we had a small TV and they didn't even speak English where it was happening so I knew it wouldn't hurt us. We were safe.

And I remember twenty-five years later watching a theatre show in Melbourne with a woman who had lived in Chernobyl telling us she had been standing on a train platform when the explosion happened, on her way to law school.

Then she laughed I remember, onstage, and she looked over our heads off to the side, you know, where people look when they are somewhere else inside, and she said 'That's right, I wanted to be a lawyer'. But then she said the minute she heard about the explosion she never went home again.

Actually, that play was about Sarajevo.

I remember the wind at the top of a phone tower I climbed once in the middle of the night. I was all alone and I wanted to see the sky.

I remember climbing the rungs, one after the other, for what seemed an entire lifetime. I remember the wind was so strong my clothes stuck hard to my legs so I took off my undies, at the top of the tower, to let myself breathe. I remember my flaps, and that I could feel them in the wind, as they started to move. I remember my flaps started to feel like they were speaking, like they were singing, no more than singing … yodelling! Yes, my flaps were Julie Andrews at the top of that hill in Switzerland with the mountaintops—and I know it was Switzerland not Austria, because my flaps were so free, not like in the movie when she stood on those hills at the start and still had the whole film to get through, with the soldiers coming and the Von Trapps, no, it was like after the film, that's how my flaps were—it was like arms-outstretched-Julie-Andrews-in-the-hilltops, but free and no longer a nun, and this was before Julie lost her voice, she lost her voice I remember, it was nodules, they needed to operate and she was left with permanent damage, but this was before all of that, this was when my flaps still had their four-octave range, my flaps were still green, and verdant, and moist, and alive, so open, so expansive, and I've never felt that way again, not ever!

I remember the footage of Tiananmen Square and the death of Princess Di and when Paul Keating became Prime Minister of Australia. I don't remember voting. I remember marching for refugees, and marriage equality, and Indigenous rights. I remember vigils.

I remember the plane that went down. I remember going on a date with a man who knew a woman who knew a man on the plane that went down. He said to me, 'It could be worse, the woman desperately wanted a family, and she finally fell in love when she was thirty-seven years old, and they went to Europe to celebrate their engagement, but she had to fly home early for work and he came back on the plane that went down'.

My memory from that plane was those three kids and their grandfather.

It could be worse.

I remember Russia. I remember vodka and dirty statues and drunk Australians in hostels.

I remember dance classes on wooden floors in old Melbourne dance studios when I was new to the city and looking for friends.

I remember I used to like gin.

I remember offending people. I remember the look on her face.

I remember being told to 'stop over thinking everything' and to 'just have fun' and not knowing how to do that.

I remember Brixton. And St Petersburg. And Hong Kong. Singapore. I remember Utrecht and Vienna and Budapest. I remember Amsterdam in summer. I remember Amsterdam in winter. I remember Sydney and Auckland, Brisbane, Perth, Darwin, those freshwater rockpools out of town, I remember Kakadu, faintly. Uluru. I remember Toowoomba. Byron Bay, Christchurch. Brighton (when it was cold). I remember a muddy island festival off the coast of the UK but I do NOT remember the hat I wore despite the photos. I remember queuing for the portaloo, and a woman in front of me turning around and saying, 'You know, people say it can be fun to be at a music festival in the rain, but it's actually just really shit'.

I remember desperately needing coffee.

I remember when I was so scared of talking to new people that my collarbone would throb and rise up and my eyes would strain open and my contact lenses would pop out on the ground.

I remember being laughed at. I remember making people laugh.

I remember the taste of strawberries the first time I went to England when I was twenty-seven years old, and how they tasted exactly the way I'd always imagined strawberries would taste and realising that I'd never really tasted strawberries before, even though when I was fourteen my best friend and I went picking strawberries in the South Australian countryside in the middle of summer and we ate them straight off the vine.

Is that what it's called? A strawberry vine? Or is it a bush?

I remember seeing art and I remember not wanting to like it.

I remember the first time I failed. I remember the second time I failed.

I remember conversations after midnight when our two brains knitted together for hours and hours as if they were one and I remember not knowing afterwards if it had ever really even happened or if I'd just wanted it to.

I remember the bad sex much more than I remember the good sex. Is this normal?

I remember Rotterdam, and Brussels. I remember Bangkok and Peshawar. I remember the border to Afghanistan, the men with the guns and the women and children without them. I remember Dubai, many, many, many, many times. I remember the capital of Sweden, and Riga. I remember Stuttgart and Berlin. I remember Muscat, in Oman. I remember Rome … from before I was born. I remember the Holocaust and those camps in Poland. I remember the grey mud and the mist. I remember Warsaw and Krakow and drinking hot beer out of plastic straws. I remember climbing a mountain in Cape Town. I remember a cliffside road trip with my fiancé and the fresh fish we ate and the bed in the motel we rented. I remember a pub on the Great Ocean Road and those huge rocks towering out of the ocean and falling over in the wind.

I remember Los Angeles, where I've never been.

I remember a theatre performance I saw that went on and on and on. There was no beginning. Not much of a plot. Just talking. It was about race, or class, or … something important.

I remember the raw carrot sticks and asparagus I ordered from the theatre cafe beforehand, which was the only thing on the menu I could afford. I remember the teenager who stumbled into the foyer out of the cold after the play had ended; he was wasted, tumbling into the wall, propping himself up against it, looking at the ground as we all walked past him. I don't think he knew where he was.

I remember a long string of fake pearls given to me in Primary School by a boy called Jean-Paul Victory. I remember the name, Jean-Paul Victory, but I don't remember much else about him.

I remember a blind boy in class called Toby who went on to be quite successful, I think.

I remember my ten year high school reunion. I was at Richard's funeral that morning. Richard's best friend Ben was the first boy I'd ever kissed. I remember seeing the first boy I'd ever kissed for the first time in a decade, at his best friend's funeral, on the morning of my ten year high school reunion.

Richard wasn't insane, he was depressed. I had another friend who was insane. I think she had a personality disorder.

I remember I used to bake every weekend. I remember I used to clean things, and run ten kilometres, and believe in myself.

I remember I used to believe in every single one of you.

I remember reading an interview with a scientist who thought that perhaps the aliens are controlling their own little fun park here on earth, and maybe they just push a button when they get bored and watch the meltdown, which might be a big earthquake somewhere or a tsunami … I remember he said, ‘How wonderful it might be if this was true. It takes the pressure off somehow don’t you think? If we aren’t in control of it all?’

But also I think how stupid it is of the aliens to keep pushing the same buttons, why is it always Afghanistan and Syria and the Philippines and South America. When will they hit Sydney? Oh wait …

I remember a young Rastafarian sat down next to me one day on a tram in Melbourne. He showed me his poetry which was all about the devils who run the world who were always gonna keep him down and I said I don’t agree, I think that in their heart of hearts people just want to be good. So the Rastafarian pulled his phone out and he showed me a video taken in a refugee camp in Africa.

He showed me footage of a huge pile of rubbish surrounded by people, standing in a circle, and on top of the pile of rubbish were human beings, human rubbishes, human bodies barely alive, so weak they could barely be called human really, and all of a sudden one of them was set alight, someone threw a lighter onto a young boy who was lying on the top of this pile, and immediately the boy came alive, he jumped up from the pile and started leaping around, arms flailing in the air, all of him on fire, and some of the people in the video ran away in fright from this dancing boy, his flames unpredictable, but there were other men and women and children on the screen who were just standing around, watching it all, watching the young boy in the centre, as he ended.

‘That’s what people are really like’, said the Rastafarian.

I remember Pussy Riot, and *Treaty*.

I remember the history books I started and never finished.

I remember being locked in a suitcase. I remember lashing out.

I remember Whitney Houston, and Cindy Lauper, and Archie Roach.

I remember my hair used to be shorter. Like a boy’s.

I remember the house that collapsed in a flood.

I remember a woman in Kerala, and her wifi kept cutting out, and I found that really annoying. I found her really annoying.

I remember a cockroach on my heater in the living room and I took a shoe and went WHOOMP. It died right away.

I remember my mother telling me how many years she could afford to stay alive, on her super.

I remember a neighbour who was killed right next door, by her lover, with a knife. I didn't hear a thing.

I remember a boy I knew who died from some kind of genetic illness. He was very young when he died, maybe twenty-two, but this was many years after we all expected him to.

I do not remember my grandfather, he died before I was born. I do not remember my grandmother, even though she lived until her eighties. I remember the colour of the walls in a room where I had a one-night stand in Glasgow in 2007.

2.

An extended moment.

[*The extended moment is an opportunity for the performer, and audience, to reset to the present moment. It could be vocal or physical. In the first season of the work, this was achieved by a chanting meditation, like so: 'Does anyone know the seed meditation? If you want, you can join in. Lam—Vam—Ram—Yam—Hum—Ohm—Suyam—'*]

I remember [*describes something the peformer did this morning*].

I remember [*describes something they did an hour ago*].

I remember [*describes something they see right now*].

I remember [*describes something they hear right now*].

I remember [*describes something they smell right now*].

3.

I remember staying in the countryside in the middle of winter, and deciding to walk to the nearest train station, without a map. It was foggy and the sun set on the way and it took me two hours. I met some sheep and a donkey and two tractors. I was never alone.

I remember when renting a house with a backyard became too expensive.

I remember the moles on my back when they started to get ugly and the hair on my head that went grey before I turned thirty and the wart on my neck that appeared overnight, literally overnight, and I remember how disgusted I was by it, when it first appeared.

I remember sun spots and wrinkles and cysts and the whiskers on my chin and nobody warned me about any of this.

I remember growing vegetables in styrofoam crates on the windowsill.

I remember the first car I bought with my girlfriend, as a joint purchase, and both of our surnames were on the contract and that made me really happy.

I remember the saucepans Dad gave us for Christmas.

I remember losing my hearing. It took a long time to notice that it was actually happening because I'm fairly young to be going deaf and the doctors only found out after I got hit by a car.

I remember my friends moving away and losing contact.

I remember I quit drinking for a year and I started laughing all the time.

I remember not needing to talk to people so much, I remember not needing words.

I remember learning to speak code as an adult.

I remember having less money, and more money, and less again.

I remember the long days of sunshine and the summers that stretched for most of the year. People complained about the heat, but they still went to the beach.

I remember my nephew's first swimming lesson and how much he hated it.

I remember my housemate had to climb through water one day to reach her tram stop, and someone took a photo and she ended up in the paper.

I remember the sky going red and the radio saying there was no danger, but I could still smell the smoke from inside.

I remember meeting the Prime Minister at a cocktail party just before Christmas, and I was taller than him and I had nothing to say.

I remember the referendum that we held, but nobody agreed with the outcome, so we held another one, and another one, and another one, and another one, and another one, and another one.

I remember the workshops we attended to address skilled migration. I remember the whiteboards and post-its and plasticine. And everyone was invited, including the students. I remember that you mattered, you mattered, and you too, you mattered, even you mattered, WE ALL MATTERED. I mattered!!! It was beautiful. All of our seminars ran exactly to time.

I remember the bombing of Taipei.

I remember an architect I met in a bar, who was designing cities for the ocean, using bitcoin. He said 'It's the cowboys that change the world'.

I remember a gardener I met at a book club, who made two million dollars in one year just by selling potatoes.

I remember the enormous meat mounds grown on the barges out there: part-cow-part-pig-tastes-like-chicken.

I remember street parties that went for days, the naked kids in the bushes, and when everyone stopped buying nylon.

I remember the taps turning off in South Africa.

I remember the box cutter they used on the prisoners of war.

I remember my first AI, a little bauble called Tony, who would wake me each morning, with snuggles, like clockwork. Whatever happened to him?

I remember the trolleys and the pulleys and the doctors covered in sweat.

I remember leaving my husband. I remember the morning I took off my ring. I remember the years and years before this being much harder. I remember desperately wanting to be in love with him. I remember not being in love with him. I remember telling him that.

I remember him saying, 'I hate you, I hate you, I hate you'.

I remember the waters were so high one summer I had crocodiles in the front yard. Some people said they saw sharks. I slept on a bunk bed so tall that I could touch the ceiling without even straightening my arm. I stopped ironing.

I remember a close friend who went bankrupt and they put her in jail.

I remember talking about networks, everything was networked, everyone was networked. Staying connected. Finding connection. Connectivity. Connectedness. Interdependency.

We lost all direction. We were confused.

We passed the point of no return. We all became artists.

I remember when the state took our passports, so they could start scanning our skulls at the gate. It was unreal to be downsized like that, I felt so connected to the world.

No more queues.

I remember listening more to my body. To my injuries, to what feels good. For a while I was dieting because everyone was. Then I got fat because nobody cared anymore. What I looked like, the size of me, how I moved in space … it was immaterial. Nobody cared.

I remember my knees giving up and I remember getting new ones.

I remember the criminalisation of caffeine and the state protection of flowers.

I remember the kids we locked up until we ran out of land.

I remember the virtual islands we built for new industry.

I remember plugging myself into the city using the energy ports on the footpaths. Sticking my right heel into the socket. In the early models we had to stand still the whole time while we recharged, for like an hour. So we'd send messages to the people next to us, plugged in next to us, to pass the time, which is often how romances would start.

I remember the flesh and the sweat. The bright lights and the hygiene.

I remember all of the Life, I remember deciding there was too much of it.

I remember when the firestorms first started. I had a plane ticket booked for my friend's wedding in Germany, and I was too scared to use it, but the airlines wouldn't give refunds so some of my friends went anyway and it turned out they were perfectly safe. The planes flew higher than the flames.

I remember the earthquakes at Mecca, when the granite collapsed in on itself, like paper.

I remember the televised trials. I remember my cousin standing trial.

I remember getting tired.

I remember the drugs I would take to stop eating.

I remember our first black lesbian Prime Minister like it wasn't even a THING. There wasn't even a state holiday. And then I remember she got shot one day, during an international trade mission, by a radical feminist, and this made perfect sense at the time because of her conservative position on welfare. I remember the outrage and I remember it passing. I remember not caring about international trade.

I remember the dog we picked up from the side of the road.

I remember forgetting about archiving. I remember when all of us, together, forgot how to archive.

I remember one summer I got terribly ill. I slept for days at a time, I couldn't walk, I wasn't sure I would ever leave the house again. In fact, I remember being adamant that I would DEFINITELY NEVER leave the house EVER AGAIN. I was very clear about this. I became an invalid, a recluse. I had visions.

I wrote my will, by hand, in pencil. I hid it under my pillow. I never showed it to anyone.

And you know the only person I remember visiting during that time was a girl I knew from high school who I'd never even liked.

She brought yoghurt, which was sweet. The thought I mean, not the yoghurt. The yoghurt was sugar-free.

I remember the mould and the rotting trees underwater. The dykes that fell down and by dykes I mean mounds of dirt.

I remember the drownings. There were so many drownings. I lost my house, I had to move back in with my ex. I got an infection from the rising damp in my right toe, my big toenail. I tried creams and surgery. Nothing helped. I wore socks for three years.

It was awful.

I remember the trees who would scream as their skin burst alight and after awhile it became impossible to tell them apart from small children.

I remember the caves and the coves and the cliffs. The wet air and the lightning.

I remember I interviewed my mum about her childhood and I forgot to press record and I lost it all.

I didn't lose it. I mean, I just never had it.

I remember the people who started marrying their objects. Their refrigerator or their bicycle or their fruitbowl. Someone in my street fell in love with a windowsill. It seemed right somehow to acknowledge we were no longer at the centre of things. Of course there were the usual debates about principles of law and traditional values and some murders.

All the while I remember the objects and their silence.

I remember the crises and the summits and the missiles.

I remember the New York Stock Revolt. My first *revolution.* I thought it was funny at first, all those shareholders holding onto their shares, but then they started bringing guns into the boardrooms, and rational discussion became impossible, and my boss got shot in the knee.

I hid in the stationery cupboard with Barry, or Rick, I don't remember his name, Alan—maybe—he delivered the internal mail, I put my hand on his chest to remind him to breathe and I counted to three thousand, eight hundred and fifty something before I lost track.

We weren't even American.

I remember getting married a second time to my co-worker. It wasn't a marriage, technically, my second one. It was a civil union. We knocked down the dividing wall between our home offices and slept together in the staff kitchen and this was perfectly normal, it felt normal to us.

It's what everyone did. We were in love.

I remember the uniforms we all wore that were simple and affordable and ethically made.

I remember the shifting definition of 'ethically made'.

I remember going freelance. Which felt like a choice, at the time.

I remember the knocks on the door after midnight. The beetles that wouldn't stop breeding. The loss of the Arctic. The death of George Clooney.

I remember the year all the media empires collapsed and the news blackouts that followed. People were telling stories again, and believing in dreams, and holding meetings underground after sundown. My mother stopped visiting doctors because 'Where was the proof this stuff works', she said, 'For all we know they could be spies', and I forgot what our leaders looked like and what our taxes were paying for, and the fights began on the streets and people stopped going to work, and the rubbish piled up in front of our doors until the children were dancing with rats, so the government had to cancel our lifetime subscriptions and legislate for pay-per-view service, and after that all the advertising came back and with it the free press.

We were happy to pay good money for good science.

I remember a woman I met in London who told me she was still planning to have *babies*. She wasn't even *embarrassed*. 'Fuck the law', she said, 'Fuck the planet. It's. My. Right'.

I remember the parts of my body that got cut off. First the leg, after a blizzard, and then my right ear.

I remember the online motels, the hold music they'd play to make us dream Caribbean and the mystics we'd zoom with at tea time. I had a fling in one once with a woman from Norway, who was really a man in New Hampshire, and we spoke Cantonese the whole time while we fucked. It was hot.

I remember that gradually, and not easily, we started to share things.

We broke bread with the field mice. We held communion. We saved the Amazon.

And immediately—Eastern whipbirds. Golden whistlers—all the birds flew away to Peru.

Silver eyes. Wattlebirds.

I remember my sister's cancer. Nobody expected that. She was perfect. And then, just like that. *Wham*. She was gone.

Spine Bills. Wedge-tailed Eagles. Western Bristlebirds.

I remember the crazy things people would do with those driverless cars. The system overrides you could find online to make them donut and cartwheel and how easy it was to be this stupid. Everyone knew someone who had seen one explode.

Sulphur-crested cockatoos.

I remember the years and years and years of construction with closed tunnels and walkways loud machinery no footpaths alternative routes traffic delays protracted spends replacement bus services political scandals public outrage

delays delays delays more delays delays delays delays more delays delays delays acts of god, deaths, explosions and new tenders

and I remember this went on for maybe fifteen maybe twenty maybe sixty thousand years and over all this time they were building under us and over us huge concrete highways stretching all across the country and by country I mean Planet Earth, of course, I mean Nation Earth. Nation World. And I remember the day these highways were finally finished and we ran out into the streets in the middle of the day wearing only our gumboots to look at the sky and we celebrated with champagne and hoots and Mexican waves because we felt something was finally over you know, something somehow had finally been achieved.

But then also I remember we didn't even notice it happening.

Crimson topaz. Harpy eagles. Lyrebirds.

I remember packing up my mother's house. I still look like her, even today.

Black Falcons. Southern Boobooks. Tawny frogmouth. Willie Wagtails.

I remember the night my wife asked for a divorce. She said she'd fallen in love. Just like that, fallen in love, as if this was easy to do. I refused to accept it. I remember yelling 'I hate you, I hate you, I hate you'.

Night Parrots. Hooded Robins. Black-eared miners. Mallee emu-wren. Eastern grassowls. Dusky moorhen. Western gerygone. Pigeons. Straw-necked ibis. Fan-tailed cuckoo. Forest ravens. Pelicans and nankeen kestrels.

I remember trashing my photos one drunken afternoon because the file names didn't mean anything to me anymore, just reams of jpegs taking up space with random strings of numbers and dates and times of the day. What was the need for a memory like this, I thought. *I want to DE-BUG. I want to be clean. I want to be free again to know NOTHING.*

Pause.

I remember the first funerals on Mars.

I remember the infants they found in the storm drains.

I remember the pain in my kidneys. The coins we would hide under the bed.

The Rastafarian saying—'That's what people are really like'.

I remember my breasts, and his bones.

I remember this thing called time, it was cheaper back then, than it is today. I was three hundred years old when I swam my first marathon.

I remember the growth underfoot and the dew where I was buried.

I remember the cosmos

and the lights from the stars, including the biggest one, the sun.

I remember where the light came from and how it travelled and refracted and I remember when we started to catch it to make it stronger and louder and hotter. I remember we discovered where love came from and how to manufacture it, we discovered our intestines, how they worked and our inner realities, what they meant and we worked out how to talk about all this complicated stuff called our feelings.

I remember we took all this light and this love and we added it to other known superpowers of the universe like air pressure, and gravity. And mathematical symmetries. Relativity. Thermodynamics. Behavioural psychology. Base physical impulses. The yearning. The abyss. There were the ones who found solutions and the ones who found a way to convince us. And we started to listen again. We started to listen again. All of these carved-out, cleaned-up pockets of truth, we stitched them together and strung them out in ways that made it possible for us to finally carry truth without words.

A silence, at least fifteen seconds.

A physical and sonic score starts gently and sweetly, as if you already know this song, it's a story you know well, almost too well it's naff, perhaps we are disappointed by how naff it sounds like a bedtime story or nursery rhyme, but the score continues, it deepens, layer upon layer, until gradually it becomes something quite else, there might be new instruments or other sounds perhaps not musical, it might be at times painful or uncomfortable, the score becomes many things at once with a constant forward momentum, and continues for at least five minutes while the actor continues in a repeatable physical score that is physically demanding but entirely free and without pain. We should feel a sense of release or catharsis, while the rhythm of the physical score should be guided by laws of the universe such as entropy and gravity and the human breath and then, abruptly, like a meat cleaver hitting the butcher's block—

BLACKOUT.

Melbourne Theatre Company

BOARD OF MANAGEMENT
Chair Patricia Faulkner AO
Martin Hosking
Tony Johnson
Larry Kamener
Katerina Kapobassis
Professor Duncan Maskell
Sally Noonan
Chris Oliver-Taylor
Leigh O'Neill
Tiriki Onus
Anne-Louise Sarks
Tania Seary
Craig Semple
Professor Marie Sierra

FOUNDATION BOARD
Chair Tania Seary
Deputy Chair
Jennifer Darbyshire
Jane Grover
Sally Lansbury
Sally Noonan
Hilary Scott
Rupert Sherwood
Tracey Sisson

EXECUTIVE MANAGEMENT
Artistic Director & Co-CEO
Anne-Louise Sarks
Executive Director & Co-CEO
Sally Noonan
Executive Producer & Deputy CEO
Martina Murray
Artistic Administrator
Olivia Brewer

ARTISTIC
Resident Director
Tasnim Hossain
Head of New Work
Jennifer Medway
New Work Associate
Zoey Dawson
New Work Associate (leave cover)
Mark Wilson
Playwriting Fellow
Jean Tong

CASTING
Casting Director
Janine Snape

PRODUCING
Senior Producer
Stephen Moore
Company Manager
Julia Smith
Deputy Company Manager
Lachlan Steel

DEVELOPMENT
Director of Development
Rupert Sherwood
Senior Philanthropy Manager
Sophie Boardley
Annual Giving Manager
Meaghan Donaldson
Philanthropy Coordinator
Emily Jenik
Business Development Manager
José Ortiz
Partnerships Manager
Portia Atkins
Partnerships Coordinator
Isobel Lake

EDUCATION & FAMILIES
Director of Families & Education
Jeremy Rice
Learning Manager
Nick Tranter
Education Content Producer
Emily Doyle
Education Coordinator
Brodi Purtill

PEOPLE & CULTURE
Director of People & Culture
Sean Jameson
People & Culture Business Partners
Christine Verginis
Tom Lambert
Receptionist
David Zierk

FINANCE & IT
Director of Finance & IT
Rob Pratt
Finance Manager
Andrew Slee
Assistant Accountant
Nicole Chong
IT & Systems Manager
Michael Schuettke
IT Support Officer
Darren Snowdon
Payroll Officer
Julia Godinho
Payments Officer
Harper St Clair
Building Services Manager
Adrian Aderhold

MARKETING & COMMUNICATIONS
Marketing Manager
Rebecca Lawrence
Marketing Campaign Managers
Grace Gaylard
Ashlee Read
Marketing & Communications Coordinator
Matisse Knight
Digital Engagement Manager
Jane Sutherland
Digital Coordinator
Isabelle Wawrzon
Lead Graphic Designer/Art Director
Kate Francis
Content Designer
Sarah Ridgway-Cross
Editorial Content Producer
Paige Farrell
Editorial Content Producer (leave cover)
Tilly Graovac
Publicity Consultant
Good Humans PR

PRODUCTION
Technical & Production Director
Adam J Howe
Senior Production Manager
Michele Preshaw
Production Manager
Jess Maguire
Production Administrator
Alyson Brown
Technical Manager – Lighting & Sound
Kerry Saxby
Senior Production Technician Coordinator
Allan Hirons
Production Technician Coordinator
Nick Wollan
Production Technician Operators
Marcus Cook
Max Wilkie
Production Technicians
Stella Dandolo
Claire Ferguson
Scott McAllister
Lila Neiswanger
Gemma Rowe
Ounie Witherow Aitken
Technical Manager – Staging & Design
Andrew Bellchambers
Production Design Coordinator
Jacob Battista
Head Mechanist
Bryn Cullen
CAD Drafting
Max Bowyer

PROPERTIES
Properties Supervisor
Geoff McGregor
Props Maker
Colin Penn

SCENIC ART
Scenic Art Supervisor
Shane Dunn
Scenic Artists
Alison Crawford
Colin Harman

WORKSHOP
Workshop Supervisor
Andrew Weavers
Set Makers
Sarah Hall
Nick Gray
Philip De Mulder
Peter Rosa
Simon Juliff
Welder
Ken Best

COSTUME
Costume Manager
Kate Seeley
Costume Staff
Jocelyn Creed
Lyn Molloy
John Van Gastel
Costume Coordinator
Carletta Childs
Millinery
Phillip Rhodes
Costume Hire
Liz Symons
Costume Maintenance
Jodi Hope
Claire Munnings
Art Finishing
Alicia Aulsebrook

STAGE MANAGEMENT
Head of Stage Management
Whitney McNamara
Resident Stage Manager
Ben Cooper
Stage Managers
Rain Iyahen
Annah Jacobs
Liam Murray
Brittany Stock
Pippa Wright

SOUTHBANK THEATRE
Theatre Manager
Mark D Wheeler
Events Manager
Mandy Jones
Production Services Manager
Frank Stoffels
Front of House Manager
Drew Thomson
Lighting Supervisor
Geoff Adams-Walsh
Deputy Lighting Supervisor
Tom Roach
Sound Supervisor
Joy Weng
Deputy Sound Supervisor
Will Patterson
Fly Supervisor
Sean Waite
Deputy Fly Supervisor
Callum O'Connor
Stage & Technical Staff
Jon Bargen
Ash Basham
Al Brill
Suzy Brooks
Connor Brown
Emily Campbell
Steve Campbell
Will Campbell
Bryan Chin
Kit Cunneen
Jeremy Fowlie
Tallulah Gordon
Kylie Hammond
Adam Hanley
Justin Heaton
Spencer Herd
Chris Hubbard
Ethan Hunter
Louis Kennedy
Julia Knibbs
Marcus Macris
Alexandre Malta
Jason Markoutsas
Terry McKibbin
David Membery
Sharna Murphy
Lila Neiswanger
James Paul
George Richardson
Jake Rogers
Natalya Shield
Jim Stenson
Nathaniel Sy
Tom Vulcan
Dylan Wainwright-Berrell
Tom Willis
House Supervisors
George Abbott
Tanya Batt
Matt Bertram
Sarah Branton
Kasey Gambling
House Attendants
Rhiannon Atkinson-Howatt
Stephanie Barham
Emily Busch
Briannah Borg
Zak Brown
Sam Diamond
Liz Drummond
Leila Gerges
Bear
Hugo Gutteridge
Abby Hampton
Michael Hart
Elise Jansen
Kathryn Joy
Natasha Milton
Ernesto Munoz
Ben Nichol
Brooke Painter
Lucy Pembroke
Brigid Quonoey
Taylor Reece
Adam Rogers
Solomon Rumble
Sophie Scott
Mieke Singh
Ayesha Tauseef
Olivia Walker
Alison Wheeldon
Rhian Wilson

TICKETING
Director of Ticketing Operations
Brenna Sotiropoulos
Customer Service Sales Manager
Jessie Phillips
VIP Ticketing Officer
Michael Bingham
Education & Ticketing Officer
Mellita Ilich
Subscriptions & Telemarketing Team Leader
Peter Dowd
Box Office Supervisors
Bridget Mackey
Tain Stangret
Box Office Supervisor (leave cover)
Darcy Fleming
Box Office Attendants
Tanya Batt
Sarah Branton
Britt Ferry
Kasey Gambling
Min Kingham
Julia Landberg
Evan Lawson
Julie Leung
Lee Threadgold
Rhian Wilson
Subscriptions Team Leader
Julie Leung
Subscriptions Officers
Daniel Alder
Stephanie Barham
Amy Dorner
Casey Gould
Hugo Gutteridge
Erin Hazel
Petria Hogarth
Min Kingham
Julia Landberg
Tom O'Sullivan
Isabelle Paci
Frederick Pryce
Cara Richards
Molly Webb

CRM & AUDIENCE INSIGHTS
Director of CRM & Audience Insights
Jerry Hodgins
Database Specialist
Ben Gu
Data Analyst
Sionna Maple

ARTISTIC ASSOCIATES
Tony Briggs
Zoë Coombs Marr
Patricia Cornelius
Roshelle Fong
Kate Hood
Paul Jackson
Margot Morales
Stephen Nicolazzo
Zindzi Okenyo
Corey Saylor-Brunskill
Amy Sole
Sonya Suares

COMMISSIONS
The Joan & Peter Clemenger Commissions
Kylie Coolwell
NEXT STAGE Commissions
Kamarra Bell-Wykes
Angus Cerini
Claire G Coleman
Patricia Cornelius
Roshelle Fong
Declan Furber Gillick
Dan Giovannoni
Sheridan Harbridge
Elise Esther Hearst
Matt Heffernen
Andrea James
Claudia Karvan
Phil Kavanagh
Benjamin Law
Kirsty Marillier
Nathan Maynard
Glenn Moorhouse
Kate Mulvany
Joe Penhall
Leah Purcell
Chris Ryan
Sally Sara
Melanie Tait
Aran Thangaratnam
Megan Washington
Mark Winter

OVERSEAS REPRESENTATIVE
New York
Kevin Emrick

Our Donors

We gratefully acknowledge the ongoing support of our leading Donors.

LIFETIME PATRONS

Acknowledging a lifetime of extraordinary support.

Rowland Ball OAM and
The Late Monica Maughan
Pat Burke
Peter Clemenger AO and
The Late Joan Clemenger AO

The Late Greig Gailey and
The Late Dr Geraldine Lazarus
Allan Myers AC KC
and Maria Myers AC
The Late Biddy Ponsford
The Late Dr Roger Riordan AM

Maureen Wheeler AO
and Tony Wheeler AO
The Late Ursula Whiteside
Caroline Young and
Derek Young AM

ENDOWMENT FUND DONORS

Supporting Melbourne Theatre Company's long term sustainability and creative future.

Leading Gifts

Jane Hansen AO and
Paul Little AO
The Late Max Schultz and
The Late Jill Schultz
The University of Melbourne

$50,000+

The Late Margaret Anne Brien
Tony and Janine Burgess
The Late Geoffrey Cohen AM
The Late Valerie Gwendolyn King
The Late Biddy Ponsford
Andrew Sisson AO and
Tracey Sisson
The John & Myriam Wylie
Foundation

$20,000+

Robert A. Dunster
Tania Seary and Chris Lynch

$10,000+

Tony and Nathalie Johnson
Jane Kunstler

$5,000

Anonymous (1)

$2,500+

Anonymous (1)

$1,000+

Xue Snowe Li

PLAYWRIGHTS GIVING CIRCLE

Supporting the NEXT STAGE Writers' Program, our industry-leading commissioning initiative.

Paul and Wendy Bonnici & Family, Tony and Janine Burgess, Kathleen Canfell, Fitzpatrick Sykes Family Foundation, Jane Hansen AO and Paul Little AO, Larry Kamener and Petra Kamener, The Margaret Lawrence Bequest, Helen Nicolay, Tania Seary and Chris Lynch, Craig Semple, Dr Richard Simmie

TRUSTS & FOUNDATIONS

The Gailey Lazarus Foundation

Annual giving

Acknowledging Donors whose recent gifts help enrich and transform lives through the magic of theatre.

BENEFACTORS CIRCLE

$50,000+

Krystyna Campbell-Pretty AM
Peter Clemenger AO
Fitzpatrick Sykes Family Foundation
Jane Hansen AO and Paul Little AO
Andrew Sisson AO and Tracey Sisson ●
Maureen Wheeler AO and Tony Wheeler AO

$20,000+

Alan and Mary-Louise Archibald Foundation ●
Edith Burgess
Tony and Janine Burgess
The Margaret Lawrence Bequest
Tania Seary and Chris Lynch
Craig Semple

$10,000+

Joanna Baevski ●
John and Lorraine Bates
Jay Bethell and Peter Smart
The Late Dr Jane Bird
Michael Buxton AM and Janet Buxton
Kathleen Canfell
The Cattermole Family
The Cordiner Family ●
Jennifer Darbyshire and David Walker
John and Joan Grigg OAM
Linda Herd ●
Tony and Nathalie Johnson
Petra and Larry Kamener
Daryl Kendrick and Leong Lai Peng (Betty)
Suzanne Kirkham
Macgeorge Bequest
Ian and Margaret McKellar
Helen Nicolay
Pimlico Foundation
Catherine Quealy
Janet Reid OAM and Allan Reid
Lisa Ring
Anne and Mark Robertson OAM ●
Dr Richard Simmie
Rob Stewart and Lisa Dowd ●
Three Springs Foundation
Ralph Ward-Ambler AM and Barbara Ward-Ambler
Matt Williams – Artem Group
Anonymous (2)

$5,000+

Bagôt Gjergja Foundation
James Best and Doris Young
Paul and Wendy Bonnici and Family
Bowness Family Foundation
Dr Douglas Brown and Treena Brown
Dr Andrew Buchanan and Peter Darcy
Ian and Jillian Buchanan
Bill Burdett AM and Sandra Burdett
Lynne and Rob Burgess
Pat Burke and Jan Nolan
Diana Burleigh
Alison and John Cameron
Ann Cutts
Prof Glyn Davis AC and Prof Margaret Gardner AC
The Dowd Foundation
Roger and Jan Goldsmith
Lesley Griffin
David and Lily Harris
Jane Hemstritch AO
Tony Hillery and Warwick Eddington
Bruce and Mary Humphries
Sam and Jacky Hupert
Dr Sonay Hussein, in memory of Prof David Penington AC
Amy and Paul Jasper
Josephine and Graham Kraehe AO
Jane Kunstler
Glenda and Greg Lewin AM
Helen Lynch AM and Helen Bauer
Martin and Melissa McIntosh
Paula McKinnon
Kim and Peter Monk
George and Rosa Morstyn
MRB Foundation
Tom and Ruth O'Dea ■
Leigh O'Neill
Dr Kia Pajouhesh (Smile Solutions)
Bruce Parncutt AO
Christopher Reed
Renzella Family
Lynne Sherwood
Tintagel Bay P/L
Marion Webster AM
Janet Whiting AM and Phil Lukies
Anonymous (7)

PROGRAM GIVING CIRCLES ■ YOUTH AMBASSADORS ● EDUCATION

ADVOCATES CIRCLE

$2,500+

Ros Boyce
Jenny and Stephen Charles AO
Geoff Cosgriff ●
Susanne Dahn
Ann Darby ●
Megan Davis and Antony Isaacson
The Dodge Family Foundation
Rodney Dux
Melody and Jonathan Feder
Anna and John Field
Jan and Rob Flew
Nigel and Cathy Garrard
Diana and Murray Gerstman
Charles Gillies and Penny Allen
Heather and Bob Glindemann OAM
Henry Gold
Jane Grover
Halina Lewenberg Charitable Foundation
Peter and Halina Jacobsen
Leg Up Foundation ■
Lording Family Foundation
Virginia Lovett and Rose Hiscock
Professor Duncan Maskell and Dr Sarah Maskell
Margaret and John Mason OAM
Don and Sue Matthews
Sandra Murdoch
Jane and Andrew Murray
The Myer Foundation ●
Nelson Bros Funeral Services
The Orloff Family Charitable Trust
Roger and Ruth Parker
Jeremy Ruskin and Roz Zalewski
In memory of Marysia and Berek Segan AM OBE
Prof Barry Sheehan and Pamela Waller
Brian Snape AM and Christina Martin
Geoff Steinicke
Ricci Swart AM
James and Anne Syme
Richard and Debra Tegoni ●
Liz Tromans
The Veith Foundation
Price and Christine Williams
The Ray and Margaret Wilson Foundation
Gillian and Tony Wood
Anonymous (4)

LOYALTY CIRCLE

$1,000+

Prof Noel Alpins AM and Sylvia Alpins
Margaret Astbury
Ian Baker and Cheryl Saunders
John and Dagnija Balmford
Prof Robin Batterham
Sandra Beanham
Angelina Beninati
Judy Bourke ●
Steve and Terry Bracks AM
Jenny and Lucinda Brash
Bernadette Broberg
Nigel and Sheena Broughton
Beth Brown and The Late Tom Bruce AM
Nan Brown
Rob and Sal Bruce
Julie Burke
Katie Burke
Geoffrey Bush and Michael Riordan
Pam Caldwell
Helen and Dugald Campbell
John and Jan Campbell
Jessica Canning
Clare Carlson
Fiona Caro
Chernov Family
Assoc Prof Lyn Clearihan AM and Dr Anthony Palmer
Sandy and Yvonne Constantine
Barry and Deborah Conyngham ●
Karen Cusack
Natasha Davies
Sue and John Denmead
Dr Anthony Dortimer and Jillian Dortimer
Robert Drake
Mark Duckworth PSM and Lauren Mosso
Dr Sally Duguid and Dr David Tingay
Pam Durrant
Bev and Geoff Edwards
Karen and David Ellas
George and Eva Ermer
Anne Evans and Graham Evans AO
Marian Evans
Dr Alastair Fearn
Peter Fearnside and Roxane Hislop
Peter and Mary Fildes
Grant Fisher and Helen Bird ●
Rosemary Forbes and Ian Hocking
Bruce Freeman ■
Dr Justin Friebel and Jessica Rose
John R Fullerton
Gaye and John Gaylard
Christine Gilbertson
Gill Family Foundation
Fiona Griffiths and Tony Osmond
Ian and Wendy Haines
Charles Harkin
M D Harper
Mark and Jennifer Hayes ●
Luke Heagerty
Lorraine Hendrata
Brett and Kerri Hereward
Dr Alice Hill and Mark Nicholson
Emeritus Prof Andrea Hull AO
Nanette Hunter
Ann and Tony Hyams AM
Will and Jennie Irving
Karen Inge and Dr George Janko
Peter Jaffe and Judy Gold
Neil Jens ●
Ben Johnson and Mark McNamara
Ed and Margaret Johnson
Sally and Rod Johnstone
Lesley and Ian Jones
Leah Kaplan and Barry Levy
Irene Kearsey and Michael Ridley
Malcolm Kemp
Daniel Kilby
Fiona Kirwan-Hamilton and Brett Parkin
Doris and Steve Klein
Marianne and Arthur Klepfisz
Larry Kornhauser and Natalya Gill ● ■
Anne Le Huray
Verona Lea
Alison Leslie
Peter and Judy Loney
Lord Family
Kerryn Lowe and Raphael Arndt

PROGRAM GIVING CIRCLES ■ YOUTH AMBASSADORS ● EDUCATION

Elizabeth Lyons
Ken and Jan Mackinnon
Karin MacNab
Natasha and Laurence Mandie
Chris and Bruce Maple
Ian and Judi Marshman
Lesley Mason
Penelope McEniry
Heather and Simon McKeon ■
Garry McLean
Libby McMeekin
Emeritus Prof Peter McPhee AM
Rosemary Meagher and The Late Douglas Meagher
Robert and Helena Mestrovic
Ann Miller AM
Ross and Judy Milne-Pott
MK Futures
Barbara and David Mushin
Sarah Nguyen
Nick Nichola and Ingrid Moyle
Dr Paul Nisselle AM and Sue Nisselle
Sally Noonan
David and Lisa Oertle
Dr Jane and Alan Oppenheim
Arthur Ozols
In loving memory of Richard Park
Dr Annamarie Perlesz
Peter Philpott and Robert Ratcliffe
Philip and Gayle Raftery
David Reckenberg and Dale Bradbury
Sally Redlich
Victoria Redwood
Veronica and John Rickard ●
Phillip Riggio
Ken and Gail Roche ●
Roslyn and Richard Rogers Family ●
S and S Rogerson
B and J Rollason
Sue Rose
Nick and Rowena Rudge
Jenny Russo
Edwina Sahhar
Margaret Sahhar AM
Alex & Brady Scanlon Giving Fund
Sally and Tim Scott
Jacky and Rupert Sherwood
Diane Silk
Dr John Sime
Pauline and Tony Simioni
Jan Simon
Jane Simon and Peter Cox
Tim and Angela Smith
Annette Smorgon
Dr Ross and Helen Stillwell
Rosemary Stipanov
The Stobart Strauss Foundation
Irene and John Sutton
Christopher Swan ●
Rodney and Aviva Taft
Frank Tisher OAM and Dr Miriam Tisher
John and Anna van Weel
Graham Wademan and Michael Bowden
Walter and Gertie Wagner ●
Kevin and Elizabeth Walsh ■
Pinky Watson
Kaye and John de Wijn ●
Ann and Alan Wilkinson ●
Robert and Diana Wilson
Ralph Wollner and The Hon Kirsty Macmillan SC
Mandy and Edward Yencken
Anonymous (25)

LEGACY CIRCLE

Acknowledging supporters who have made the visionary gesture of including a gift to Melbourne Theatre Company in their will.

John and Lorraine Bates
Mark and Tamara Boldiston
Bernadette Broberg
Adam and Donna Cusack-Muller
Anne Evans and Graham Evans AO
Bruce Freeman
Peter and Betty Game
Edith Gordon
Fiona Griffiths
Linda Herd
Tony Hillery and Warwick Eddington
Jane Kunstler
Irene Kearsey
Robyn and Maurice Lichter
Dr Andrew McAliece and Dr Richard Simmie
Libby McMeekin
Peter Philpott and Robert Ratcliffe
Marcus Pettinato
Jillian Smith
Diane Tweeddale
Anonymous (17)

PROGRAM GIVING CIRCLES ■ **YOUTH AMBASSADORS** ● **EDUCATION**

Current as of January 2024. For more information about supporting Melbourne Theatre Company please contact our Philanthropy team at donations@mtc.com.au or visit mtc.com.au/support

Thank you

Melbourne Theatre Company would like to thank the following organisations for their generous support.

Major Partner

Future Directors Initiative Partner

MinterEllison.

Major Marketing Partner

The Monthly
The Saturday Paper
7am

Associate Partners

Supporting Partners

southgate

Marketing Partners

Southbank Theatre Partners

SCOTCHMANS HILL
BELLARINE PENINSULA
VICTORIA
ESTABLISHED 1982

Current as of April 2024. To learn more about partnership opportunities at Melbourne Theatre Company or to host a private event, please contact partnerships@mtc.com.au

MELBOURNE THEATRE COMPANY PLAYS

PUBLISHED BY CURRENCY PRESS

37

Nathan Maynard

The local footy team of this small coastal town have spent so long at the bottom of the ladder they might as well be welded to it. This year a new hope arrives: the Marngrook cousins are named after the Aboriginal game that inspired AFL, and they're match fit to bring home the team's first flag in forever. Penned by Nathan Maynard – twice named Tasmanian Aboriginal Artist of the Year – *37* is a reminder that honest conversations are more than a ball toss. It matters where you stand.

978-1-76062-892-5, available in print

MY SISTER JILL

Patricia Cornelius

A universal tale of the Australian spirit set against the backdrop of 1950s to 70s suburban Melbourne, *My Sister Jill* is a powerful coming-of-age story from one of the country's most dynamic theatre collaborations, Patricia Cornelius and Susie Dee. The youngest in the family, Christine idolises her father, especially his stories of wartime heroics. Her sister Jill, meanwhile, doesn't quite share the same sentiments. As the intensity of the Vietnam War looms, the stories slowly start to lose their shine and war threatens to break a new generation apart. At once compelling, captivating and ultimately hopeful, *My Sister Jill* has all the makings of an Australian classic.

978-1-76062-823-9, available in print

JACKY

Declan Furber Gillick

'Do you have anything at all that's actually yours? That's actually real?'
Jacky is a smart, enterprising young blackfella in the big city. He skilfully negotiates the gig economy, skipping neatly from office internships

to cultural performances to sex work. When his unemployable little brother Keith rolls into town, Jacky's carefully compartmentalised lives are set to collide. Declan Furber Gillick is an Arrernte writer and artist from Mparntwe (Alice Springs) with a practice spanning theatre, television, poetry, music, rap and visual arts. In 2018 he took up a residency with Melbourne Theatre Company's NEXT STAGE Program. *Jacky* is Declan's debut with the company.

978-1-76062-822-2, available in print

A VERY JEWISH CHRISTMAS CAROL
Elise Esther Hearst with Phillip Kavanagh

Local baker Ely is not letting anything get in the way of fulfilling customer demand for her Bubi's famous Polish gingerbread. Not her family's impending Chrismukkah celebrations; not the imminent birth of her child; and certainly not the ghosts who've suddenly shown up in her kitchen. But the Rein-Dybbuck of Chrismukkah Past, Gingerbread Golem and Lilith Claus have other ideas… Drawn from the writers' own backgrounds, *A Very Jewish Christmas Carol* is a celebration of life—with a sprinkle of time-travelling ghosts, overbearing relatives and a life lesson or two.

978-1-76062-824-6, available in print

LAURINDA
Diana Nguyen with Petra Kalive

Adapting Alice Pung's award-winning book, writer and comedian Diana Nguyen and director Petra Kalive bring Laurinda's schoolyard setting to the stage for a fresh and feisty new work. Like *Heathers* or *Mean Girls* with a uniquely Australian flavour, this delightful take on the beloved novel is an incisive, funny study of a woman caught between cultures and class. When 15-year-old Lucy Lam wins the inaugural Equal Access Scholarship to a prestigious private school, the smart and well-liked student is not prepared for the new world she's suddenly propelled into. It's a world of wealth and opportunity, overseen by The Cabinet—a trio of girls who wield power over their classmates, and even their teachers. But when The Cabinet turn their attention to Lucy she has to make a choice: fit in and succeed, or stay true to herself. Either way, there's a cost. Whether high school is (thankfully) a distant memory or a current reality, this MTC NEXT STAGE commission offers a witty and moving insight into an all-too common experience as well as the inner strength it takes to speak truth to power.

978-1-76062-781-2, also available as an ebook

SLAP. BANG. KISS.
Dan Giovannoni

SLAP. A video of 16-year-old Immi hitting a security officer goes viral. BANG. Sofia's impassioned speech for the victims of a school shooting makes international news. KISS. In the car park of a small-town Woolies, people rally around Darby and Daniel as the boys lock lips in an attempt to set the world record for the longest kiss. Shortlisted for the 2021 Victorian Premier's Literary Awards and included on the VCE Drama Playlist for 2022, this new play is from multi-award-winning playwright Dan Giovannoni (Merciless Gods). *SLAP. BANG. KISS.* tracks three young people whose stories kickstart a series of events none of them could have anticipated, transforming them into global symbols of revolution. But when their stories go viral and the whole world is watching, what will they do next?

978-1-76062-773-7, also available as an ebook

PRIMA FACIE
Suzie Miller

Top criminal lawyer Tessa believes in the law, she believes in the system, she believes in playing by the rules. If you play by the rules, justice will be served. She has not only staked her career on these principles, she has placed her very faith in them. But when the tables are turned and Tessa has to take the witness stand, she is forced to confront the shortcomings of the legal system and its patriarchal foundations of justice. In the multi-award-winning play *Prima Facie*, Suzie Miller delivers a one-woman tour de force—by turns wryly amusing and powerfully shocking—that exposes the failings of a system seemingly designed to further brutalise women who have experienced sexual assault, rape or harassment. For Tessa, as for so many women, truth turns out to be less about reality and more about how you play the game. And in this court, nobody wins. *Prima Facie* won Best New Play at both the Olivier Awards and the WhatsOnStage Awards in 2023, as well as the 2020 AWG Best Play Award, the David Williamson Prize, and the Major AWGIE award.

978-1-76062-841-3, also available as an ebook

THE HEARTBREAK CHOIR
Aidan Fennessy

From the revered playwright behind one of Melbourne Theatre Company's most beloved hits, *The Architect*, comes this funny and uplifting celebration of music, friendship and community. *The Heartbreak Choir* is a warm-hearted hug of a play that will make you want to sing out loud. In the old CFA hall on the outskirts of town, a small group of locals come together to sing, and to connect. Aseni, Barbara, Mack, Savannah and Totty have splintered from their original choir on a matter of principle and are intent on forging their own path. With their latest recruit Peter along for the ride, they have a new name, a space to rehearse in and a public debut booked. All they need now is to right the wrongs of the past … and to find a song that pairs perfectly with the local winery's Sangiovese. This joyful, song-filled snapshot of a devastated community learning how to heal is the last work from playwright Aidan Fennessy—a fitting final act of togetherness.

978-1-76062-776-8, also available as an ebook

SUNSHINE SUPER GIRL
Andrea James

A grimy old ball, a racquet made from a wooden fruit box, a pair of borrowed shoes … then the world at her feet. This is the heart-warming story of how Evonne Goolagong Cawley—our Evonne—rose from humble beginnings in an outback farming town to become a world-champion tennis player by the age of just 19. With a tin wall for a court and a steely determination, little Evonne hits and hits and hits her way out of rural New South Wales and onto the world stage. On the way she must battle prejudice and homesickness and test herself to the very limits. *Sunshine Super Girl*, by Yorta Yorta/Gunaikurnai writer Andrea James, is a funny and poignant take on the life of a talented sportswoman with a big dream. Infused with a wry Australian sensibility and a proud sense of belonging, it's a story that will inspire and delight.

978-1-76062-675-4, also available as an ebook

MELBOURNE TALAM

Rashma N Kalsie

'I have completely lost my talam. All I hear is the ring of mobile phones, the noise of escalators, platform announcements and the trains squealing on the tracks. Where's the koyal, where's the ring of temple bells, where's Carnatic music, where's my mother's voice?' Three young people see each other across a crowded Flagstaff station. They just missed the train. Now they wait. And think. They think about home: Punjab, Delhi, Hyderabad. And about how they just can't seem to get Melbourne's rhythm right. And of all the impossible things they must do to stay. And their time is running out. Developed through MTC CONNECT and the NEON and Cybec Electric play development programs, this vibrant play puts Melbourne's contemporary social issues at centre stage.

978-1-76062-085-1, also available as an ebook

BERLIN

Joanna Murray-Smith

Charlotte is a Berliner through and through. Tom is a foreigner, travelling around Europe. After meeting in a bar, sparks fly between them and she invites him to spend the night at her place. As they navigate the ritual of seduction, their desire gives way to secrets that cannot be ignored and questions neither of them can answer. Does young love stand a chance against the suffocating reach of the past? Joanna Murray-Smith is one of Australia's most celebrated playwrights, captivating audiences from Melbourne to Broadway and the West End. A powerful mix of thriller, romance and ethical dilemma, Berlin will keep you guessing until the very end.

978-1-76062-802-4, also available as an ebook

OTHER PLAYS BY CURRENCY PRESS

HOLDING THE MAN
Tommy Murphy

Holding the Man is based on Timothy Conigrave's celebrated memoir of the same name, which won the 1995 UN Human Rights Award for Non-Fiction and was voted one of Australia's top 100 favourite books. Tommy Murphy's stage adaptation faithfully captures the book's heart-wrenchingly honest portrayal of a fifteen-year relationship, but also succeeds in transforming it into a unique theatrical experience that is wholly his own. The play won multiple awards and had seasons across Australia and internationally.

978-1-76062-887-1, also available as an ebook

DRIZZLE BOY
Ryan Enniss

'Bugger. Maybe you aren't Rain Man. Maybe you're more of a Drizzle Boy.' Drizzle Boy loves space. So does his companion, Space Bear, and his hero, Russian cosmonaut Valentina Tereshkova. The stars are far away from a world that unforgivingly pokes and prods him. Until Drizzle Boy is brought back to earth by Juliet, who enters his orbit on the first day of university. How does one figure out romance, when social etiquette already seems arbitrary? Who makes the rules? Who enforces them? And why should any of that matter, when your world is conjoined with the vast infinitude of outer space? Ryan Enniss' award-winning Drizzle Boy is the first Australian play written by an autistic playwright about an autistic protagonist.

978-1-76062-869-7, available in print

THE JUNGLE AND THE SEA
S. Shakthidharan and Eamon Flack

War makes things of people. *The Jungle and the Sea* is about a family who refuse to become things while they are still alive. When violence escalates between the Sinhalese-dominated Sri Lankan government and the Liberation Tigers of Tamil Eelam, a Tamil mother vows to remain blindfolded until her family is together once again. Gowrie, Abi and Madhu search the jungles of northern Sri Lanka for estranged son Ahilan, while Siva and Lakshmi migrate to Australia for safety, awaiting their family's reunion. Separated by the ravages of civil war but buoyed by humour, playfulness and love for each other, so goes the story of many a migrant family that has wound up in Australia. Co-writers S. Shakthidharan and Eamon Flack continue their collaboration that began with *Counting and Cracking*, threading personal testimony from the Sri Lankan civil war with two ancient epics — the *Mahabharatha* and Sophocles' *Antigone*. The war may have ended in 2009, but Tamil memory endures in *The Jungle and the Sea*, calling together lives that eternally revolve, intertwine and bear witness to each other.

978-1-76062-851-2, also available as an ebook

RAINBOW'S END
Jane Harrison

'We're second-class citizens in our own country. No, we're not even citizens. Heavens, and this is the fifties!' History is about the heroes. *Rainbow's End* chronicles the lives of three generations of Koori women —unsung heroes who fight the good fight every day from their humpy on Yorta Yorta country. Matriarch Nan Dear, the emerging activist Gladys, and the aspiring nurse Dolly reside along a river that continues to rise, threatening their displacement (time and time again). Faced with subtle, and not so subtle, racism in their daily lives, the Dear women stand their ground. Jane Harrison's *Rainbow's End* is, above all, a story of how radical change unfolds in the most quotidian of exchanges, in the love shared by Aboriginal women within their families and their communities.

978-1-76062-850-5, also available as an ebook